402

Guidelines for Courtship
&
Preparation for Marriage

by Jeff Barth

First Edition - 1995
Revised Second Edition - 1996

The Barth Families - 1996

Betsy (Andy's wife) & Andy - 23, Marge & Jeff, Beth - 17, Joe - 19, Charity - 20
Dorcas (Ben's wife) holding Annette - 1 & Ben - 26 holding Peter - 2

The Barths live in beautiful northern Vermont where they moved over 19 yrs. ago to begin their home schooling career. Jeff & Marge have 5 children, ages 17-26, as well as 2 grandchildren. Their 2 oldest sons, Ben & Andy, have both apprenticed under their Dad in Dental Technology, now have their own dental lab businesses, and have both gone through courtship. Ben has been married for 3 yrs. to a lovely young lady named Dorcas who is also from a "pioneer" home schooling family of 9 children, and they have a precious 2 yr. old son named Peter & a darling 1 yr. old daughter named Annette. Andy went through courtship last year and was married in December of '95 to a precious young lady named Betsy who is also from a home schooling family of 9 children.

Many families are exploring Biblical Courtship alternatives to replace the heartbreaking dating game used in the past decades. Having now passed through the process of courtship with their 2 oldest sons, the Barths share from experience in this booklet the essential aspects to courtship, as well as important qualities for preparing sons & daughters for marriage.

Guidelines for Courtship
&
Preparation for Marriage

Our eldest son, Ben, is now 26, has gone through courtship, and has been married for over 3 years to Dorcas. They have been blessed with a 2 year old son, Peter, & a 1 year old daughter, Annette, and are "expecting" in February of '97; both Ben & Dorcas attended Christian schools through the third grade and were then exclusively home educated. Our second son, Andy, is 23, has always been home schooled, has also gone through courtship, and was married in December of '95 to precious Betsy; and they are "expecting" in early November of '96. Our oldest daughter Charity is 20, our youngest son Joe is 19, & our youngest daughter Beth is 17; so all of our children have attained (or are soon approaching) a marriageable age. Therefore we have given much thought to a Biblical approach to courtship & marriage, and with Ben & Andy each being now married, we have some personal experience to draw from as well.

It's true that parents often learn the most in child rearing with their firstborn, not only in child training, but in every area of life. God was gracious in giving us a good bit of success and Biblical wisdom and insight through the process of Ben & Dorcas's courtship & marriage, and now we have the added blessing of Andy & Betsy's courtship & marriage. Overall their courtships were extremely rewarding, but as with anything in life, once you have some experience, you know more what to look for and expect. In this booklet, I would like to discuss some major topics that parents should focus on in preparing their sons & daughters for courtship & marriage, but before I do, let me give a brief description of what makes courtship different from dating.

What Makes Courtship Different from Dating?

There are several elements which make courtship different from and more Biblical than the cultural practice of dating.

1st The main element that makes courtship different from dating is that it involves parental input, counsel, and guidance from both sides of the relationship; whereas dating generally does not consider parental advice as necessary or important. We have the example of several successful marriages in Scripture where details of the pre-marriage period are described; each has some kind of parental or authority input involved such as: Isaac & Rebekah, Jacob & Rachal, and Boaz & Ruth. Contrasting to these successful examples, we see with Samson what may be considered a clear example of our modern cultural practice of dating, and the struggles that may come to a marriage when parental or authority counsel is rejected. In fact, in Scripture we do not find a single example of what might be considered a successful relationship resulting from a dating type arrangement (i.e - Samson, Dinah, Esau, and Genesis 6:1-3).

2nd Unlike the often temporary design of dating, courtship is primarily intended to be the beginnings of a permanent relationship: it should be entered into with each side having the intentions that the purpose for the courtship is that it may consummate in a marriage.

3rd Courtship is a giving, covenanted relationship where each partner and family on each side is working together to help the young couple grow in oneness of spirit and heart.

4th Courtship includes the counsel of parents so that together with their young person, they may find God's perfect gift, that one person God has designed to complete their young person. It involves more than just finding a Godly young person for theirs.

5th Courtship involves parental guidance and input in planning the activities and chaperoning as necessary. Parents often know best, during this period the couple shares together before marriage, the weaknesses of their young person and can help their young people avoid the temptations which are frequently a part of a dating relationship.

Why Use the Term - Courtship?

As our children were reaching the mid to late teen years, we didn't have any particular term in mind for describing this process of our young people meeting and marrying their life partners. All Marge & I knew from our past was that we were going to avoid the struggles, temptations, and emotional scars which frequently are a part of the dating game. Several years ago, we began hearing the term "courtship" being passed around, and so it caught on with us. In recent years some are taking issue with this term "courtship", contending that they have heard of couples entering into courtship and then ending up breaking up and starting a new courtship with someone else. Isn't this the same as "dating around"? Not really - mainly for the reason that parental counsel is involved in courtship. However, some have come up with alternative terms for courtship that supposedly will more solidify the commitments which a couple may make for marriage. One such term being suggested is "betrothal". We do feel that betrothal or engagement should be the final step of commitment in a courtship before the actual marriage takes place, but we do not see that by simply changing the terms used that we come up with a more secure or more Biblical relationship. In fact, we have recently heard of a young couple who preferred calling their relationship betrothal which ended up breaking up.

The Christian life is a life of faith. We all attempt to make the wisest decisions we can in life, praying and hoping that we are truly discerning God's perfect will for us and our children in any given situation; but we still live by faith and understand there is an element of risk in decisions we make in life. James suggests that we can not always make a definitive decision in regards to our future. "Come now you who say today or tomorrow we will go into such a city, and continue there a year and buy and sell, and get gain...Instead you ought to say, 'If the Lord wills, we shall live and do this or that' " - James 4:13, 15. I believe it is more or less immaterial what we actually call this pre-marriage period. The most important issue isn't the term used to define it, but more importantly what goes into it.

What's Wrong With "Breaking Up"?

We live in a culture that does not see the dangers of the "breaking up" mentality which prevails today, even among Christians. We live in a divorce prone society, and many believe (and I am in agreement) that this divorce mentality has been a direct result of dating, particularly among those who dated around. Those who have dated around in their teens and early twenties have been more conditioned to "breaking up" than they have been to "being faithful". How does this work? A common theory with teens who date is that if they find some incompatibility with their partner, that they "break up" in hopes of finding that "perfect one". A young person who has gone through a series of dating partners has been conditioned to breaking up when something arises, rather than trying to work through difficulties. Many good, God-ordained marriages today have ended up dissolved simply because these couples have been conditioned to breaking up by this pattern of dating around from their teen years. Futhermore, dating around also sometimes nurtures a callousness in the heart of a young person where they grow cautious of wanting to yield their total heart to their life partner, simply because they have been hurt so many times in the past by dating partners who left them.

There are some specific steps we can follow to minimize the potential of breaking up. Let me suggest a few considerations:

1st Parental involvement on both sides is by far the most important element in minimizing the potential for break up. If parents on either side have an immediate "check" or caution over the relationship, things should be approached very cautiously, or stopped, or delayed until everyone feels a true peace. Once parents allow emotional bonding to begin taking place between their young persons, it is often very difficult and painful emotionally to interrupt what has been allowed to begin.

2nd A young person should not attempt to get halfhearted or a hasty approval from parents on either side. Many break ups occur because parents thought they were obligated to give a hurried response or approval before they came to a fairly secure peace about a relationship. However, I would like to add this - that sometimes the "true colors" of another young person are not fully known until after a relationship is allowed to initially begin. Sometimes a young person's true character comes out more once things have been allowed to get started a little.

> *God's "perfect gift" for your young person will bring out the best in your young person.*

During the earliest days of a courtship, each young person should be very yielded to the guidance and discretion of their parents and be willing to accept their more objective discernment. Parents play a protective role in the lives of their children, and they can keep their young person from a painful and disheartening future.

3rd Remember, parents, that courtship is more than just attempting to find another Godly young person for yours to marry. It involves finding and discerning God's perfect gift for your young person, that perfect one. God's perfect "gift" for your young person will bring out the best in your young person, but a counterfeit will make you somewhat discouraged with what you are seeing in yours. So give sufficient time and prayer in making your evaluation before you give approval for a courtship to begin, and don't let it start until you all have a reasonable "peace" about things.

By approaching a potential relationship with discernment, prayer, and caution, we can many times avoid the heartbreaks of breaking up. However, if we do experience a break up, this does not mean the quality of God's future relationships for us will be forever spoiled or at least, as some would have us to believe, unable to reach their full potential for God. Rather, God can graciously use our past experiences sometimes to help us recognize and greatly appreciate even more His perfect gift when he or she does, indeed, come along.

In summary, the most important thing in courtship is not the term we use to describe the process of a young person meeting their life partner, but much more importantly what goes into it. So what all is involved in the courtship process? We see, basically, 3 periods prior to the actual marriage. I would like to explore each of these periods in some depth.

First, there is the *Pre-courtship Period*. In this period, the young person generally does not have another young person in mind for marriage. This is primarily a season for the young person to experience growth in the areas of character, vocation, Biblical wisdom and spirituality. It is important during this period that the young people protect their thought life from planning, hoping for or developing feelings towards another. They must learn to evaluate others, including potential marriage partners, closely with their parents.

Following this period after sufficient maturity in vocational training, character development and spiritual growth relating to marriage has occurred, and after God brings along a potential marriage partner (assuming the relationship has the approval of all parental authorities and the young man and woman involved) a *Courtship Period* now follows. Of course, no one can set an exact age when courtship plans should begin, but we would recommend a minimum age range of around at least 20.

Some today are beginning to take issue with this term "courtship" because in some circles the concept of courting is again beginning to drift back into a dating type lifestyle. We want to carefully guard against this possibility, because now that the novelty of this "courting" is beginning to wear off, Christian young people can begin dating in the world's sense and conceal this by calling it Christian Courtship. Courtship is not a period where young people flippantly or in the least bit lightly enter into a relationship. This Courtship Period must be very carefully entered into. Parents on both sides must give prayerful consideration to their feelings and cautions, and if any parent feels a caution or fear over the potential relationship, the Courtship Period should be put off until these feelings are reasonably satisfied and there is a "peace" on the part of the parental counselors.

Neither should any courtship arrangement be initiated without the understanding that this Courtship Period is intended to consummate with a marriage, that being the whole purpose for it. We do not want to allow courting to drift into a dating type arrangement where a young person is just experimenting with a relationship for a while; courtship should be approached very seriously by all. However, it is still somewhat of a "trial" period even though it is basically assumed by parents and young people that no foreseeable problems will arise (there is that minute possibility during this period). I believe the

> *Once the Engagement or Bethrothal Period is entered into, a much deeper sense of oneness in spirit is now experienced between the couple.*

important element here, to prevent things from getting started and then having problems arise, is for parents not to allow things to even begin without feeling pretty confident about the relationship.

Following this Courtship Period and as the young people and parents alike grow in confidence over the developing relationship, there will now follow a third *Engagement* or *Betrothal Period*. This begins when the young man actually asks the young lady to marry him. However, before the young man formally makes this request, he should once again go to his future in-laws as well as his own parents and gain a final approval or blessing. This is a faith building period for young people. Once the Engagement or Betrothal Period is entered into, a much deeper sense of oneness in spirit is now experienced between the couple as they can confidently arrange and make plans for their future together. During this period, it is extremely unlikely and very remote that the marriage would be called off at some point. Some would liken a separation during this period nearly or actually to the point of divorce, and I think that does speak of the seriousness of this period. I would like to explore each of these periods in some depth.

Don't Encourage Dating Or A Dating Spirit

As parents, Marge and I knew years ago that we would never consider allowing our children to date in the world's sense of dating around. We realized from our worldly upbringing that this kind of dabbling not only hurts the emotions and esteem of young people and puts them in situations of temptation, but it is also clear training for divorce. As I have already shared, the concept of dating around says that if you are unsatisfied with certain characteristics in another then you try another relationship with hopes it will be more compatible. This kind of mentality, trained into a young person's life for several years through dating, is preparing them for marriage problems or divorce. Mature Christians know that we must work through differences and problems, not abandon our partner.

However, it is very important for our young person to be able to wisely, along with their parents and under parental authority, discern the character of others. This character evaluation must begin long before any kind of a boy-girl relationship begins, whether it is called courtship, getting acquainted, or just being friends with hopes this will grow into a lasting relationship. In a sense, dating is also a way of evaluating the character of others, but dating often carries the flaw in reasoning which says that we are not really serious about this person becoming our life partner. This kind of playing with relationships creates youthful passion and emotions, and is warned against in Scripture. "Flee also youthful lusts." (II Tim. 2:22) Dating promotes youthful passion, but a dating spirit can be nurtured in youth without them ever dating around, and a dating spirit can present just as many negatives as actual dating.

What Is A Dating Spirit?

A dating spirit is acquired by having a regular interaction or involvement with others on an emotional level that either intentionally or unintentionally excites or plays on youthful desires, passions or emotions. A dating spirit is similar to what some call being flirtatious; it is a kind of friendliness that attempts to attract another young person in emotional ways. The only problem is that, due to the drift in the morals of our society, what was once considered flirting is now called just being friendly, even in Christian circles.

The Scriptures teach daughters to be discreet in their actions and conduct—not bold, independent nor "Miss Personality" in demeanor. (See I Tim. 2:9.) A flirtatious girl would not be modest in conduct. Instead, she would feel a freedom to converse or interact with various other boys; unknowingly, this independent friendliness often attracts boys and is a kind of "dating spirit." Of course, boys can be flirtatious also and inappropriately play on a maid's emotional responses by drawing a girl along. For this reason, daughters should be encouraged to bring to their parents' attention any advances she may encounter from a young man. She should also be taught to direct an advancing young man to her father first, thus keeping herself under her father's spiritual protection and discernment. The same would be true for boys who are confronted with advancing girls. Boaz praised Ruth for this virtuous quality of "following not young men, neither poor or rich." (See Ruth 3:10.) Boaz and Ruth recognized the inappropriateness of this kind of friendly dating spirit that young people sometimes engage in to attract a mate.

Young people need to be taught not to initiate or respond to these emotional approaches from another young person until they are actually ready or close to being ready for courtship, and they have approval of this person by their parental authorities. Young people need to be taught to keep the level of interaction and conversation with other young people on more of a brief greeting, friendship level or a dating spirit can arise. Attraction can even be conveyed through such simple things as eye contact, being in a room together, playing some kind of game or sport, and during youth get-togethers. Even a girl being off alone can attract or convey a dating spirit.

Youthful passion is very addicting to young people, and once they have tasted this kind of emotional friendliness with others, they will greatly desire this, sometimes even to the point of excluding their own parents and family. This sometimes leads to rebellion in youth. My wife and I were careful not to allow our teens to get into these regular youth involvements that could fuel these youthful desires and draw them away from a closeness with us. At first, we thought we were really "off" with this conviction, but we knew the teen group was a very common practice in the world and among worldly Christians, so it seemed probably true that God must have in mind a much purer and less tempting way for young people to get acquainted. We are now seeing the beautiful fruit of our decision, how carefully our older ones have passed through those years of youthful temptations, how self-controlled they are, and how soberly they look at marriage.

Bear in mind also that the greatest attraction between a man and a woman, even greater than apparel, make-up, and hair styles, etc., is created by sharing conversation. The deeper the conversation, the deeper the attraction. Both the "froward man" and the "strange woman" use flattering speech or praise to attract others into conversation. (See Proverbs 6:12-13, 5:3 and 7:5.) They both also display somewhat of an independent lifestyle. We need to train our sons and daughters to be alert to these mannerisms of those who are displaying this kind of attracting, dating spirit. Some try to justify this kind of friendliness among Christian young people, saying they are just brothers and sisters in the Lord, and as long as the young person has pure motives, there will be little temptation. This is partly true, and some conversation is okay; but I believe too much of this on a regular basis can lead to youthful temptations. Furthermore, youth who are allowed to have this freedom of friendliness with various young men or ladies tend to continue this practice after they are married, feeling a freedom to converse with other married Christian men or women of the opposite gender. This is a vivid practice in the world around us in every fiber of our society. This freedom of friendliness, conversation and interaction is seen in the co-ed classroom, co-ed work environment and our co-ed society as a whole, and is one of the root causes of moral decline in our country. The Christian approach should be to use discretion and set a better example for the world around us.

> *The greatest attraction between a man and woman... is created by sharing coversation.*

I believe Paul's directives for a man not to "touch" a woman is addressing this issue. "It is good for a man not to touch a woman." (See I Cor. 7:1,2.) This word "touch" in Greek in general conveys nothing too deep or overly intimate, but it also means "to kindle." It is talking about a casual encounter that is frequently a part of everyday life in our society, which may kindle feelings. Paul says it's good not to have too much of this contact; it can lead to greater temptations. He also knew that some of this would be unavoidable, and there is wisdom in trying to keep this contact at a minimum between Christians in Christian social situations.

We do not want to tempt our young person (or ourselves) with these passions through wrong involvements or interactions, but we do want to provide some opportunity for them to become acquainted with others of suitable character for life partners. They are going to have to have some opportunities to meet and to begin having feelings for another young person. This presents a very real problem to many families and brings us to our second point of consideration.

Parent/Youth Involvement Together In Evaluating Character Of Others

One of the most important aspects in child training is helping our young person evaluate the character of others. By character, I mean such things as lifestyle, modesty, morality, worldliness, fleshliness, etc. When our children are young, we do this for them by keeping them from social contact that will present negative influences so they won't learn the negatives. As our children get older, we teach them the wisdom (most of the Proverbs are given to us to help us discern the character of others) of why we are avoiding regular contacts with certain individuals or things. So, over the years, we develop a team approach in evaluating life with our children, and this should continue and be a vital part of teen training. Nurturing this kind of parent/young person cooperation and closeness in evaluating others is essential in successfully finding a Godly life partner.

> *One of the most important aspects of child training is helping our young person evaluate the character of others.*

My wife and I realized we needed to direct our sons to those families we thought had suitable character that we would consider desirable to develop relationships with. It didn't take us long, however, to realize that such families were few and far between. Many families are discovering this to be true.

There was a time in Christian culture when the church was the place to find other families of similar conviction and lifestyle. But now that many Christian parents have stepped out and have begun setting a new standard that emphasizes the Godly unified home and principles that lead to this end, they are having trouble many times finding suitable marriage partners for their sons and daughters within their churches. Parents have begun exploring other options for meeting others of likemind. Parents are sending their children to colleges, encouraging them to get involved in youth type organizations or programs, and encouraging other co-ed type involvement in hopes of remedying the life partner situation for their young person.

Generally, situations where the young person is "on his or her own" in finding a life partner create temptations for the young person, and the young people frequently fail to recognize the flaws in the character of others. Parents sometimes (but not always) get upset with the choice of a life partner that their young person has made. This can be avoided if a team approach is used in this important aspect of life.

Samson was on his own when he met his first wife from Timnath, and you will recall that Samson's first marriage to this woman was never blessed and ended in a terrible tragedy. (See Judges 14.) "And Samson went down to Timnath (he was alone), and saw a woman in Timnath of the daughters of the Philistines. and he came up, and told his father and his mother, and said, 'I have seen a woman in Timnath of the daughters of the Philistines: now therefore get her for me to wife.'" Evidently, even in the troubled days of the judges, it was customary for parents to be involved to some degree in arranging a marriage.

The text then tells us that Samson's parents did not feel right about this particular woman, and they pled with Samson to reconsider. "Then his father and mother said unto him, 'Is there never a woman among the daughters of thy brethren, or among all my people, that thou goest to take a wife of the uncircumcised Philistines?'" (Judges 14:3) However, at this point, Samson's emotional involvement with this woman had already preempted his own sense of reason as well as his parents' counsel, and Samson said to his father, "Get her for me; for she pleaseth me well..." Another translation of this phrase puts it this way: "Get her for me. She's the right one for me." NIV. There are times when a young person becomes so emotionally attached to another, that they convince themselves that this is their God-ordained life partner even when, as in this case, it is obviously not true.

As a family, we carefully avoided "joining" something, thinking this would solve the marriage partner need of our sons and daughters. We wanted God to work this out for us. We did try to befriend other families of similar convictions as ours, but we have not sent our young people away to college or something similar with this in mind. We have concerns about the independent lifestyle that young people sometimes acquire when away at college, particularly for girls, and would encourage apprenticeship or correspondence college study instead. There was a time in early American history when college preparation was thought only desirable for young men, and I think there is some real wisdom in reasoning such as this.

Similarly, we would not encourage our daughters to be ministering on their own. Of course, the age of the unmarried daughter should be considered here. Perhaps an unmarried daughter in her mid-to-late twenties may have more freedom than a young daughter. But, in general, the woman's ministry described in the Bible is clearly a supportive role to the man (her father or husband). The woman's ministry was a hidden ministry, particularly in the younger years.

Older women were encouraged to teach younger women, but most of this teaching to the younger was designed to direct them back into their own homes, seeing their husband and children as their first ministry for Christ. The only women encouraged in ministry were presumably "older women" who could wisely teach younger women in areas of discretion, chastity and being responsible keepers at home. Godly homemaking is a full time Christian ministry for young Christian wives and mothers.

So what are some ways our young people can get acquainted with others of suitable character? I can say this—don't panic or, in desperation, try working this out in your own efforts. Let God work a miracle. Both Ben & Dorcas and Andy & Betsy wondered as they were getting older how they would ever meet someone of suitable character. All of our families had led rather separate lives, but when the time came for our children to marry, God worked out the circumstances for our families to meet. We would suggest getting together with other families of similar convictions. This is a desirable way for young people to meet and get acquainted. In such circumstances, the character of the young person is displayed to the parents on both sides. Some kinds of family involvements such as camp meetings, home schooling family retreats, or other involvements where likeminded families are together can also provide opportunities to meet others.

Young people should be of sufficient age and maturity before they should be allowed or encouraged to give much thought to courtship needs. We feel 20 would be the minimum age before a young person should be encouraged with courtship. It seems unlikely that a young man would be prepared sufficiently vocationally to provide for a wife and a family much before 20, though this could be possible. Parents can usually sense when their young person is getting mature enough to consider courtship and marriage. So the first step is to evaluate the character of others together as a family and allow God the opportunity to bring us together with other families of suitable lifestyle and character for our young person. Many times finding just one other family of likemindedness is quite an accomplishment today, but God will work this out in His omniscient way and timing. We can testify to this.

Training Young People to Rule Their Emotions

One of the tragedies of "dating around" is that it often leaves emotional scars in the lives of the young people. How can much of this be avoided? First of all, we must realize that life itself has emotional letdowns in it from time to time; this is part of life to some extent, and we can't expect to avoid this entirely. Many years ago when our 8 year old daughter's favorite bunny suddenly died, she grieved because she didn't even get to say "good-bye"...we all had some tears for awhile when our son's foal, who we had raised and all gotten attached to, died unexpectedly... and when the plans we had made to move to another state finally fell through, we were all letdown for awhile, too. So a normal amount of emotional grief or letdown will be a part of all of our lives to some extent, but some emotional grief can turn into emotional scars that we can carry with us if we will not work through our past feelings and leave them behind us.

Ruth could have very well carried emotional scars and feelings from her first marriage, but both she and her mother-in-law, Naomi, (although at first in heaviness) eventually overcame these feelings. All of us need to be able to overcome and forget the past, resigning emotions and experiences as something God allowed, but that are now behind us. Learning to "die" to a vision or an attachment of some kind is important for all of us to be able to do; this is part of not letting our emotions control our lives.

Young people can become emotionally attached to one another rather easily if they are not careful to rule their emotions. When I was in public school, everyone knew when "so and so" had a "crush" on "so and so". This word "crush" was the word we used to define this carefree emotional attachment that was growing between two young people; but a young person doesn't have to go to school to work up this kind of emotions for another person. Sometimes just by meeting another family, or receiving a letter or picture, a young person can begin building up a relationship in their mind and their emotions.

It is wise to train young people to be careful not to do this. Of course, when we do encounter another family with prospective young people, it is easy to begin to wonder if another young person might be the right one for ours, and our young people can easily begin thinking this way, too. At this point, it's very important to keep these possibilities only on the surface of our emotions, and to caution our young people to not start building up things in their minds, or fabricating plans in their minds. The "fear of the Lord" comes into play here - remembering that God is bringing together in life whom He sovereignly chooses, and keeping ourselves under His will and authority. It is so easy to start getting emotionally attached long before other considerations are made such as: the other young person's spiritual and moral life, theological differences between families, character concerns, and other concerns that either set of parents may have. With all the factors involved, it's easy to see how foolish it would be to allow emotions to get too carried away, either with young people OR parents.

I see, basically, three emotional stages in a relationship. The first would be surface emotions with a willingness to easily forfeit these thoughts; these surface type of emotions should be a part of the Pre-courtship period. The second stage of emotions would occur during the actual Courtship period which may involve more emotions, but certainly reserved and constantly brought under the parental oversight because this is still somewhat of an evaluation period. In the third stage during the betrothal or engagement period, emotional bonding and life planning can begin more in earnest, but the "fear of the Lord" and His ultimate will still prevail here until the marriage date.

I believe we see in Boaz & Ruth this reservation and ruling of emotions as their friendship developed. Finally as they made plans at the threshing floor, Boaz pointed out to Ruth that he did have a near kinsman who was entitled to her first, and that only if "God wills" shall he be able to perform his part of the relationship; nearly to the actual marriage date, they both had to be somewhat prepared emotionally for things not to work out. Naomi also cautioned Ruth to "sit still, my daughter, until thou know how the matter will fall." (Ruth 3:18) Both Boaz & Ruth were wise enough to keep their emotions reasonably in check in the event God may have other plans for them. More than anything today, young people need to learn the importance of this emotional self-control, and the importance of keeping their emotions under parental supervision. Of course, parents must also learn emotional self-control and not allow themselves to get carried away with things too soon either. Even after parents give a preliminary approval, emotions must still be kept in control and in check.

Some are proposing that a daughter gives her emotions to her father for his keeping, and at a certain date, he allows her to give her emotions to a young man. This emotional keeping of the father is sometimes symbolized by a father giving the daughter a locket that he retains the key to until a certain time. It is our feeling that emotions should not pass suddenly from the father to the daughter, but gradually. It is true that a daughter's emotions or feelings in life should not be independent of her father or parents, but the daughter must also learn to "keep" or "rule" her own emotions to some extent because fathers and parents are not infallible in their decisions and may, at a later date, grow cautious over a relationship which they had given initial approval of. We would suggest that rather than involving something material like a locket, that instead the father and mother just remain very close to their daughter, helping her to keep her emotions rather contained and in line with the courtship stage she is in. The young man, as well, must contain his emotions and be prepared to give them up in the event that either his own parents or the maid's parents may begin to question or have doubts about the relationship. By sharing emotions with their parents, the young person's emotions can be more easily kept in line, and not be allowed to rule the young person's thoughts or life.

A practical illustration that might help us see how this works could be related to physical hunger. Young people will have emotions, just like they will have a physical appetite and hunger for food; and it would be unrealistic to try to tell our children that we parents will control their hunger, but rather it is a combination of them controlling their own appetite while also eating dinner when the parents decide. It doesn't give a young person self-control by telling them we are in control of their hunger, but they must learn to control themselves - and the same is true in dealing with their emotions and other human passions. It is best for both young people and parents alike to be interested and encouraged about a growing relationship while allowing emotions to grow as the certainty and reality of the relationship progresses. The young person must not allow emotional development beyond the honor and will of his or her parents, and neither beyond the honor and glory of God and His omniscient plan for their lives.

Parent/Youth Involvement in Discerning the Right Life Partner

Once we meet and build a relationship with other families of similar conviction and character, the next point of importance is working together with your young person in discerning the right life partner. When we first began to meet other families of suitable character likeness with ours, I had carried over from my past the thought that it would then be my son's role to go and approach the young lady in those families. However, when my daughters started getting a little older, I suddenly realized that I wouldn't want a young man approaching one of them without first going through me.

So then I recognized that my son needed to first approach the parents, the father in particular, of a young lady he may be interested in. Then again with my daughters, I realized how disappointing it could be to a young man interested in my daughter if I had to turn him down. So it became logical that maybe there would be times when fathers should approach other fathers in this area of courtship to protect or at least cushion the impact rejection might have on a young man. (I think it would also be permissible for a young man to approach a young lady's father, and some young men may prefer to do it this way. I see nothing Biblically wrong with this, and it may be the best way in some situations.)

However, in the Old Testament culture, the general procedure followed in marriage arrangements was for the fathers to "take" wives for their sons, and the fathers were to "give" their daughters in marriage. The fathers were very much involved in the entire process generally. As we have been growing in knowledge over this subject of Courtship, I am beginning to see, more and more, the importance of fathers being involved together in Pre-courtship considerations; this is an important function in protecting the emotions of the young people involved.

The most important point here is that both young men and young ladies need to keep themselves under their parents' authority during the entire process of evaluating and finding a life partner. A son should not be encouraged to develop feelings towards a young lady until he has his own parents' approval first of all, and then he secondly secures approval from the young lady's parents; and then, of course, the young lady's agreement is of final importance.

All parental authorities should be involved and give approval before a supervised courtship should ensue. Some societies arrange the marriages of their sons and daughters. Some societies like ours leave this up entirely to the young people. Neither of these situations is best, but rather, parents on both sides and the young people as well, need to *all* be a part of the process.

> *Both young men and ladies need to keep themselves under their parents' authority during the entire process of evaluating and finding a life*

I believe we see this in Scripture. For example, in the story of Isaac and Rebekah, Rebekah's authorities "asked the maid" if she would go with Abraham's servant. With Boaz and Ruth, the authorities were involved. Samson's pursuit of a wife, however, was clearly without parental approval; and, of course, his first marriage ended in a tragedy and the second was never blessed.

My son, Ben, followed these guidelines with Dorcas after we had met her family and began to feel encouraged about our likemindedness in convictions, character and lifestyle. Of course, because our family was always in the habit of evaluating others together, it didn't take Marge and me long to realize that there were some thoughts already being generated along the lines of boy\girl friendship. Marge and I felt good about Dorcas's family, and we could sense there was an interest on the part of our oldest son for their oldest daughter. At this point and before allowing feelings to develop any further, Marge and I felt it might be wise for me to approach Dorcas's father to see how they, "in general", felt about us. I approached Dorcas's father with the thought of the possibility of one of my sons developing a relationship with one of his daughters. We wanted to know how both he and Dorcas's mother felt about us. He felt good in his spirit about the idea, and as time went by, they felt even better about things.

It is important for a young man to highly honor his mother's evaluation of a young lady in whom he might be interested. If the mother has any "checks" in her spirit regarding the young lady, it would be wise to postpone initiating things until these concerns can be brought to rest in some way. A hastily arranged courtship may present the possibility of someone's spirit being wounded, in the event things surface on down the road that could lead to cautions or problems. This same principle of evaluation would also apply to the father towards a young man interested in his daughter. Some fathers have gone through several months of communication and evaluation of a young man before they have given their approval of a courtship arrangement.

Someone possibly could be getting the feeling that courtship has somewhat of an appearance of "arranging" a marriage. On one hand, arranging a marriage does allow for the involvement of the parents in the process; and this is good. However, "arranging" marriages by parents has often been done with the exclusion of the feelings of the young people involved. It is true that it is vitally important that parents on both sides feel good about the possible relationship, but these feelings alone should not be allowed to prescribe the relationship. This should be a mutual covenant entered into by all the parties involved, parents and young people alike.

Another source of counsel that sometimes enters the picture is from a brother or sister of the young person involved in the courtship. How important is the input of a sibling's counsel? We do not find in Scripture any situations where a sibling was used in directing a young person in courtship, although I suppose in the event of the removal of parental counsel that some form of substitute authority may be used by God to aid in such evaluation. Laban (the brother of Rebekah) and Bethuel (Rebekah's father) both said that the arrangement between Rebekah and Isaac "proceedeth from the Lord." (Gen. 24:50) But later on in the story, it seems that Laban (the brother) was beginning to be tempted to postpone things. (See verse 55.) We see no indication here that Bethuel had any doubts; at least, they weren't raised if he did. After consulting Rebekah, she felt good about going ahead with things immediately. Obviously, Laban's counsel was complicating things, rather than adding to the situation. We feel that sibling counsel is something to be careful with, and it is very unwise for young people to counsel against the parental viewpoint. Wise parents will consider the input of their young people, and wise children will show openness and honor to their parents' decisions.

After consulting with us and getting our approval, Ben started having feelings about Dorcas. They weren't emotional feelings or passion feelings but more of feelings of wanting to care for her and see her life blessed. He even began to pray God would give her a husband, but he didn't know he was to be that husband. Finally after some time and again after asking us, Ben wanted to initiate writing to Dorcas, and he began to feel like he wanted to get more acquainted with her when we were together as families. Of course, during this period he continually wanted to know how we (his mother and I) felt about Dorcas.

Ben knew that any kind of emotional development would need to have Dorcas's father's and mother's approval as well as hers, so Ben called her father and expressed his desires. Ben explained that his intentions for getting acquainted included the hopes and prospects of marriage. Ben felt writing and talking together was serious; he was not just playing with emotions or passions, and he asked her father if he had any reservations in the possibility of this developing into marriage. He gave Ben his blessing.

Both Dorcas's father and mother were fairly confident of Ben's character, lifestyle and commitment to Christian living, and they felt right about Ben. At that point, Dorcas's father informed her of Ben's interest, and he encouraged Dorcas to "consider Ben." Ben then proceeded to try to win Dorcas's heart through writing and times of conversation together. (At that time, Ben was not only mature enough spiritually and in character, but was also prepared vocationally for marriage. He was nearly 23 years old.)

Actually we never really needed to encourage Ben to seek our counsel for his life partner because he had learned through the years of his upbringing that if he honored his parents' wisdom and insight and feelings in every issue of life, things would "go well for him." "Honor thy mother and father...that it may go well with thee and thou mayest live long on the earth." (Eph. 6:3) We had helped Ben through other minor decisions in life, like the time he wanted to buy a horse of his own when he was thirteen. God blessed him for waiting several months until his Dad felt "right" about when and what horse to buy by giving him one far nicer than he ever expected.

There were other areas of counsel that he saw to be blessed when he honored our feelings, too. Through the child rearing years, point out to your young people the many times when God worked through Father or Mother for their good. This will help them appreciate and respect (honor) your counsel and feelings. Teaching your sons and daughters this team approach (parental involvement) in every issue of life helps them realize they are not "going it alone" in life. Finding a life partner is one of the major concerns, perhaps the most important concern, in life to approach "together" with your young person.

Parental involvement was also a part of the beginnings of our son Andy's courtship with Betsy. Our family met Betsy's family in the spring of '94, and we spent an evening together. Over the following summer, Marge & I kept having recurrent feelings that perhaps Betsy was the "one" for Andy. We knew that Andy had some feelings this way, but we did not encourage Andy with these feelings until I made a call to Betsy's father to discuss the possibilities of a relationship beginning.

With our families living clear across the country from each other, we were not that familiar with their involvements as a family, and Betsy could have very well been committed to another relationship; and, again, we were uncertain as to their feelings about our convictions and family life in general. So I called Betsy's father to discuss the possibilities and to discern his immediate reaction.

He felt the consideration was certainly worth praying about, and he had no immediate concerns other than the fact that as families we live across the country from each other (Betsy's family is from the state of Washington). Parents on both sides prayed over things for several weeks; and although Andy was informed of our phone conversation so that he could join us in prayer, Betsy's parents felt it best not to mention the call or Andy's feelings until they could feel securely confident that this was indeed the Lord's will for their daughter. Finally parents on both sides felt that a visit to Washington by our family would allow our families an opportunity to get better acquainted and to give Betsy's father & mother an opportunity to further evaluate Andy and our family.

We flew out to Washington in early January of '95 and spent several days in their home. We continually marveled at how God was able to bring together two families of such likemindedness living so far apart; but nothing is too hard for the Lord, and when it comes time for a son or daughter to marry, He will work miraculous circumstances to bring them together. Betsy's father and mother felt confident and impressed with what they saw in Andy, and we, in turn, felt the same way about Betsy. Shortly after this visit, Betsy's parents told her of Andy's interests which she received feeling blessed. She felt good about Andy provided that her parents felt confident and "right" about the possibility of a growing relationship. A son or daughter may have feelings at the beginning of a courtship, but it is wise and best for them to remain totally yielded to parental counsel and discernment throughout the courtship, and especially at the beginning while things are being evaluated. After Andy & Betsy's courtship began, shortly after this visit, they started to become better acquainted with each other through letter writing, and they soon discovered the fax machine.

Young people need a lot of comfort and companionship (and sometimes protecting and cushioning when things don't work out) from us parents during this period before they start courting. Above all, they need our counsel in helping them evaluate the true character of a potential partner. We must look far deeper than the surface in this evaluation. Parents have more of an objective ability to do this than their young person.

It is important for parents on both sides to feel "right" about the relationship their son or daughter is seeking or desiring. Give special consideration to the feelings of the young man's mother. I get this from Proverbs 31; the verses in this chapter were given as instructions from King Lemuel's mother to her son in evaluating a virtuous woman. Mothers can usually best evaluate the true character of a young lady her son is interested in, and she may need several conversations with the young lady. His father should also take an active part in the decision, and he should give his son the final decision and evaluation of the parental team's feelings. Parents need to be "heirs together" in this evaluation, as in all decisions in life that their family may face.

The maid's father will have special insight into the true character of a young man seeking his daughter's hand in marriage. I Cor. 7:36-38 talks about a father "...standing steadfast in his heart, having power to decree without doubt" that his daughter should not marry a particular man. I believe this passage reveals how God places in a maid's father's heart the ability to discern if she should marry in a given situation. Of course, a Christian father is not alone in his decisions in life and should "dwell with his wife according to knowledge" (I Peter 3:7) in making an evaluation of a potential young man. If his wife (the young lady's mother) feels very cautious about an approaching young man, these cautions should be given full consideration and evaluation. They could be normal motherly concerns, or they could be heart felt cautions that clearly indicate this is not the "right" relationship developing. Time often comes into play here. A maid's father and mother will need opportunities to get to know the true character and commitment of the young man. It may take time for parents to come to a "peace" about a potential young man or young lady, but it is very important that everyone involved, parents and young people both, have a peace about the union; and a hasty arrangement is usually unadvisable, although God sometimes works this way, too.

Taking Time to Evaluate Others

Let's say a young man approaches you (the young lady's father) or perhaps a father approaches another father on behalf of his son expressing interest in developing a relationship with your daughter. Perhaps you feel, in a general sense, "good" about the young man, but there arise certain "concerns" in regards to their future in which you would like to be reassured. Is it best to allow a relationship to begin, hoping that these "concerns" will be taken care of during the courtship period (perhaps even after marriage), OR should the courtship period be postponed until the parents on both sides feel more sure about things?

This is not an easy question to answer, and the answer will vary depending on the degree of the "concerns" that the parents may have. If either set of parents feels cautious about things to some degree, I see nothing wrong with an extended pre-courtship period to give time to address these "concerns" or issues. Some issues take more time to discern than others, but the important thing is that both sets of parents feel reasonably reassured about the true commitment and attention that a young person gives to these "concerns".

With the prospects and attraction of marriage involved, it is easy for a young person to put on a good "show" of being committed to change in areas of parental concern, but a "show" certainly isn't enough. For this reason, a trial period of some extent may need to be part of the picture before parents allow the courtship to actually begin.

I believe we see some evidence of this in Scripture in the life of Jacob. He was a young man who was sheltered and was somewhat of a "Mommy's boy". We see Rebekah making decisions for Jacob; for example, when she coached him with taking the blessing from Esau. And we see other incidences where she did the thinking for young Jacob. On one hand, a young man should honor and draw from his Mother's counsel; but if a young man cannot properly or responsibly lead, this may show a weakness on his part that will cause problems in his future home. I believe we can see a weakness in Jacob's character in the area of being responsible and willing to work and take a role of leadership. I sense that when Laban requested that Jacob work for him seven years for Rachel that God was working through Laban to perfect an area of character deficiency in Jacob. Later on, when Jacob fled with his wives, he said to Laban, "You changed my wages ten times, and the sleep fled from my eyes." Jacob was learning the responsibilities of handling money as well as the physical trials of disciplined work habits - perhaps two areas where his character needed improvement. It is true that these areas of character may have just as well improved after marriage, but there are times when things do not improve after marriage; in fact, they may even get worse.

God was probably working through Laban to help Jacob in these areas of character. Often we think of Laban as being an insolent person (and maybe he was to some degree), but God was also working through him for Jacob's future good. Every young person needs time to mature and to begin to learn the responsibilities of marriage, and many times the future in-laws can give a young person valuable counsel on specific areas in which to concentrate.

Heeding Parental Concerns

An important thought for parents to consider after you have "found" a possible life partner for your young person is this - does the young man you are considering for your daughter, or the young lady you are considering for your son, bring out the Godly character you are desiring to see in your own young person? Or do you have feelings that the other young person is bringing (or may bring) your son or daughter "down" in some way? If you feel the other young person is creating in yours some "negatives" that you may be concerned with, then I would approach the relationship cautiously and slowly. I would discuss these cautions as a couple; then inform your young person that you have certain "concerns", and help your young person not to get emotionally involved or entangled until you can feel more certain. In a truly God-ordained relationship each partner will compliment and strengthen the character of the other and there will be a tendency to bring out Godliness in each other; if you as a parent are sensing this potential young person is not doing this in yours, then I would heed this warning signal. This person may be a "counterfeit" who may present very serious temptations to your young person if a close relationship is encouraged or allowed to continue. If another young person is truly for yours, you will probably be thankful and pleased with what you are seeing and sensing, not cautious or concerned.

Letting God Work Out the Circumstances

I don't want to make it sound like Ben or Andy were constantly working or looking for a life partner, either. They weren't. They had learned to pretty well "go to sleep" (Adam went to sleep, and God made Eve) over the issue and to concentrate on seeking and serving the Lord with their lives. Both young people and parents need to "go to sleep" over this need as much as possible. Of course, young people can't help but to hopefully wonder when they meet another young person who is of acceptable Christian character and commitment if they

> *The young person and the parents alike should have serving Christ as their first priority.*

might be "the one." But if the Lord is truly first, as He should be, the young person and the parents alike should have serving and seeking Christ as their first priority in life.

Of course, God knows that oftentimes we can best serve Him as a team with a life partner. Most Christians marry, and I think God intended for most Christian men to serve God together with a life partner. A man needs a helpmate in living for and serving Christ, or his life and ministry may not meet the full potential for God's service. So it is very important in God's sight that He brings this helpmate to the man in some way. God will work this out. "He that findeth a wife findeth a good thing, and obtaineth favor of the Lord." (Prov. 18:22) This favor of the Lord is what God extends to a young man in arranging the circumstances for him to meet his life partner.

But how do you teach young people to be able to wait and release to God the concern and need they have in this area? Sometimes it becomes difficult for young people to wait, particularly as they begin getting into their mid-twenties. They tend to want to start taking matters into their own hands instead of waiting on the Lord. Two very important qualities go into helping them to be able to wait. First, through the younger years of the child rearing process, teach your children meekness. "Blessed are the meek; for they shall inherit the earth."

(Matthew 5:5) The meek inherit or are given from the Heavenly Father the needs of this life, the earthly things. Children and young people can be trained to be meek when we as parents do not allow them to be demanding, manipulating or asserting their wills in various manners over the years of child rearing.

Then, secondly, demonstrate to them the many times in life when you sought first the Kingdom and Christ's righteousness, and how God "added unto you the things of this life." "Seek ye first the kingdom of God and His righteousness, and all these things (that most people are striving to get) will be added unto you." In this section of Scripture, Matt. 6:25-33, Jesus repeatedly urges us to take no thought for earthly concerns. Today, Christians are constantly being taught to use their minds in areas of finances, health and other earthly concerns. It has become difficult for Christians to grasp the concept of taking no thought for such basic needs in life. So they end up using their minds in this area of finding a life partner, just like they do in other areas of life.

Now, don't get me wrong. There is a sense of evaluation and choosing what is best or wisest in the issues of life, but if we get to thinking about things constantly, we end up worrying or lusting instead of trusting and believing that God will provide in His time.

Jesus ends this sections in Matt. 6:25-33 with an interesting statement: He says, "...for tomorrow shall take thought for the things of itself." In effect, Jesus was saying there's going to come a day (tomorrow) when you will need to think about these needs, but up until that future day try to give it little anxious thought. There was a day when God put Adam to sleep, made Eve, and then brought her to Adam. There was a day when Rebekah went to draw water at a well. Little did she know that God, that day, had some life-changing plans in store for her. Isaac didn't know that day when he went out to meditate in the fields and to seek in spirit his God that he would meet his future life partner. Ruth had no idea that through making that choice to follow Naomi back to Palestine, forsaking her Moabitish land with its idolatry, and seeking first the true God of Naomi and her Godly people, that one day soon "all these earthly things" like the need for a husband would be "added unto her." Neither did the Godly man, Boaz, give much thought for his life in this area. He was even willing to give up Ruth to his near kinsman if God so ordained. Boaz was thus demonstrating that he was a very meek person, not demanding his will or desire, and his entire life clearly shows a man who "inherited" much good from God—even a virtuous wife.

For several years, I had to occasionally encourage and remind Ben & Andy to take no thought for this need for a life partner, and I am sure the same will be true for our other children. And now that we have seen God meet this need with two of our children, it encourages us to wait for Him to do it, Lord willing, for the others.

Sometimes young people have trouble waiting for a life partner because of tempting exposure such as teen groups where the talk or emphasis or underlying motives are towards boy/girl friendships, or where dating or a dating spirit is taking place even though you may not allow your young person to date. Passion or romance novels can be very tempting to youth, as well as some Christian biographies that put a lot of undue emphasis on romance. Slumber parties or similar youth involvements where the talk may drift into boyfriend/girlfriend type discussion can present temptations, too. Even constantly praying for a life partner can keep the issue so fresh in a young person's mind that he has trouble "going to sleep" over it or "taking no thought" for this need. By eliminating possible sources of temptation, parents can help their young person pass through these years without much fear or frustration in this area of life.

Preparing Young People For Marriage: Commitment, Character, & Vocation

Not all Christians marry, but most do. What are some basic qualities we would want to train into our young people to prepare them for marriage? I would say that these three points — commitment, character, and vocation — would be the most important basics in preparing your young person for a successful marriage.

Of course, it is of utmost importance that your young person marries only another who has certainly received Christ as his (or her) personal Saviour but it should go much deeper than this. There are many today who "claim" to be Christians but may not truly be in the faith or committed to Christ. Paul said that he was persuaded that the sincere (genuine) faith of Timothy's Grandmother and Mother was in Timothy also. This word persuaded means "prevailed upon, won over, convinced." It is very important that parents be persuaded convincingly of the faith in Christ of a young person interested in their son or daughter. I would urge looking for a "life of faith", somewhat of a zeal or desire in the young person's life to serve Christ. Do they show a love for Christ, other Christians and the work of the ministry?

> *These three points - commitment, character, and vocation - would be the most important basics in preparing your young person for a successful marriage.*

Actually, one of the best ways to build character that will prepare a young person for marriage is through serving Christ in his (or her) own home in those later teen years of ages 17 to 20, those years before courtship begins. Marriage requires, among other things, giving, adapting and yielding to the desires of our partner. When a young person learns to give of himself (even though he may be old enough to be "on his own") by yielding and adapting to the plans and desires of his parents, and fulfilling the menial tasks at home (like being willing to minister to younger brothers and sisters as well as ministering together as a family during the ages of 17 to 20 or older), he is learning to be ready for the adapting routines of early marriage.

On the other hand, young people who are always engaged in Christian activity away from home regularly or for extended periods are going to find settling down and being content with marriage and family life more difficult. Today Christian service has been so glamorized by emphasizing traveling, being a missionary, or having a personal ministry, that young people have trouble seeing their own marriages and homes as perhaps their first and foundational ministry for Christ, the success of which will determine how God will use them in other future ministries. I would encourage both sons and daughters that they will have a ministry together with their spouse that will beautifully fit both of their lives together. The wife will be the hidden helpmate and encourager to her husband in their ministry, and the husband will be the spokesman.

I don't find a single woman in the New Testament that was out front in a ministry, but I see many who were working quietly "behind the scenes" in a supportive role. God designed it this way. I see the virtuous woman in Proverbs 31 as a "hidden" woman whose ministry was primarily centered around her home; she was praised by her household, but her husband was known in the gates. Let's not get this switched. Some kinds of Christian service away from home may be beneficial and desirable for young men before marriage, but Paul urges the young ladies, in general, to marry and to see the home as their primary place of service. We would not encourage young, single men to engage too early in service away from home either. It was at the age of 20 that a young man went to war in the Old Testament, not 16 or 17; God knew much good, responsible character is learned and perfected at home up to this age.

We need to look at character in two general streams. First, there is basic Biblical Christian character, and then there is more specific marriage quality character as described in those passages of Scripture that address the marriage relationship. Let's look at these separately.

Basic Christian Character

There are several basic qualities I would encourage you to look for in a potential marriage partner for your son or daughter, the first and foremost being an honoring attitude. Does this young person show a good degree of respect and honor for his or her own parents? An honoring child will honor his future spouse, and the Scriptures promise that life in general will go well for him or her. For the young ladies, I would look for a subjective, meek and quiet lifestyle and mannerism. The improper woman described in Proverbs was loud (not quiet), stubborn (not subjective), and independent (her feet abideth not at home). (See Proverbs 7:11.) A contentious, challenging spirit in a daughter is also a general characteristic to be concerned with as a parent. A daughter who is meek and industrious (working willingly with her hands) around her parents' home would be excellent to find.

Specifically for the young man, I would look for one who shows a degree of properness, not friendliness, towards young ladies, a young man who cares for his mother and esteems her counsel very highly, a young man who is responsible and shows incentive to work and provide for his home, one who is diligent vocationally or in Christian service and ministry, and a young man who shows good work habits and discipline rather than slothfulness. Boaz's generally industrious, Godly, responsible character was well-known in his community, and it was said of Ruth, "...all the city of my people doth know that thou are a virtuous woman." (Ruth 3:11) Training our sons and daughters in basic Christian character such as these is important in laying a foundation for their marriages and their future.

Marriage Related Character

The most successful marriages are those where both husbands and wives fulfill their respective Scriptural roles as given in God's Word in passages like Eph. 5:25-33 and I Peter 3:1-7. Young people can have regular opportunities to fulfill these qualities in their own homes long before they marry, or they can be raised to neglect these qualities, and their future marriage will suffer proportionally until they are "learned and lived". What are some practices that parents can engage in with their young person to teach these Biblical marriage qualities?

One of the first passages has to do with communication that leads to approaching all of life in a oneness of spirit. Heartfelt communication is very important in marriage. In I Peter 3:7, we find a passage that advises the husband to live with his wife in this way. "Likewise, ye husbands, dwell with them (your wife) according to knowledge." Many times, it is difficult for husbands and wives to open up their inner selves to each other. The reason many have problems with this in their marriage is because they never learned

Heartfelt communication is very important in marriage.

to do this at home when growing up. It is a good idea for Moms and Dads to routinely (every day or so) get into the habit of having a heart to heart talk with their young person. Parents who practice this through the teen years will not only hedge against possible situations of rebellion, but also train their young person in the habit of getting their hearts opened in conversation. This will beautifully prepare them with good communication skills in their future marriages.

Along with this comes the importance of both sons and daughters learning some other marriage qualities. For example, the husband is the sanctifier in the marriage. (Eph. 5:26) He is to draw out Scriptural answers to life's daily struggles and issues; he is to "wash with the Word". Wives, in turn, are to desire to receive this counsel from their husbands in a spirit of reverence. (Eph. 5:33) Now, granted, many times we husbands don't have the necessary answers, and often husbands and wives will need to discover answers to challenges in life together; but this also encourages communication. By regularly talking with our young person and bringing in Biblical wisdom and application at the same time, we are preparing sons to have a solid supply of Biblical wisdom to help their future wives. Daughters also will learn to meekly express to their future husbands wisdom which they have learned while talking with their fathers and mothers. This establishes our young people in having a Biblical basis for decisions and issues encountered in life, which is also essential for a successful home.

This brings us to the most important quality for the daughter to have, a "meek and quiet spirit." (I Peter 3:4) A daughter who has learned to be meek instead of assertive, manipulative or contentious is well on the road to having a husband who will love her much and give himself for her. Daughters learn to perfect this type of character through the teen years by parents continually working with their daughter on these qualities. Of course, early child training up to the ages of 10 to 12 will begin to lay the foundation for this meekness, and parents should diligently discipline and correct children who are not meek in the younger years.

Another particularly important quality to teach daughters is the concept of submission which carries with it the idea of yielding to the requests of their authorities, even when they may have other ideas or plans. Some are trying to teach that submission is only necessary when a wife "agrees" with her husband's request and, of course, this would not be submission at all by definition, but simply agreeing. In a similar respect, even though the man is the leader and final decision maker in the home and marriage, he is specifically told to "give honor" to his wife's feelings; this depicts a sense of yielding on the husband's part. So we have a degree of mutual submission in marriage while at the same time trying to discern how God is working through our partner. Young people primarily learn the basics of this mutual submissiveness by trying to sense or discern how God is working through parental requirements or requests over the years. A son or daughter who learns to honor parents, adapting to parental desires and views, will be well-prepared with the necessary submissive qualities which lead to a harmonious marriage.

A mutual "giving" spirit is necessary for a good marriage, too. The man is specifically taught to love and give himself for his wife. (Eph. 5:25) However, wives are clearly described as being "made for the man". Originally the woman was created as a "helpfit" for her husband, and for the wife, the very concept of submission carries with it the idea of adapting herself to her husband. So the wife's role is clearly a role of giving herself for her husband as well.

Much of this "giving" character is learned by a young person in those teen years by such things as sons helping Mom, taking her to the grocery, showing a sense of protection and caring for her in other ways, etc. Sons need to also learn to comfort Mom emotionally and to see how she's doing from time to time, learning to comfort her with Scripture and counsel. Of course, daughters learn a similar giving servant's spirit by cheerfully serving around the home, learning to do such things as cleaning, cooking and wearing of apparel in ways that are pleasing to her father, and sharing Scriptural insights with her father by bringing them under his oversight.

Further development of a giving character is learned in young people as they prepare vocationally for marriage. A young man learns many basics in giving by realizing and being encouraged and directed by his father in vocational preparation. This giving spirit of a young man seeing himself as a giving provider for his future home is not learned in just a few weeks or months prior to marriage. Years ago, a young man began preparing himself vocationally long before his marriage, from the age of fifteen or so through the early twenties. He was well-trained in this quality of sacrificing of himself for his future home. Vocational skills are also important for a young man in the event he does not marry or marries late in life. His vocational training will provide a means to support his ministry. Learning to "bear the yoke" in vocational training conditions and prepares a young man to "bear the yoke" of marriage. A young man who is a cheerful, willing servant vocationally will likely be the same responsible servant/leader in his future marriage and home life.

> *Further development of a giving character is learned in young people as they prepare vocationally for marriage.*

Furthermore, young men who are busy preparing themselves vocationally for marriage will face much less temptation and preoccupation with boy/girl thoughts, too. We would encourage apprenticeship type training involving useful, marketable skills for young men, and preferably some kind of occupation that could be home-based and that leans towards self employment. Up until the turn of the century, most fathers were involved in farming or some other trade where they were readily available to the home. I would encourage fathers to return to this type lifestyle if at all possible.

Teaching sons financial responsibility and how to wisely use their resources while seeking counsel from parents is an important part of preparing them for marriage. The young man will, upon marriage, assume a role of being the leader and decision maker with most of their financial situations. The Scriptures clearly indicate that the husband is to live with his wife, drawing from her feelings and cautions, when making decisions in life - financial ones, too. "Likewise, ye husbands, dwell with them (your wife) according to knowledge, giving honor unto the wife (and her discernment) as unto the weaker vessel, and as being heirs together of the grace of life, that your prayers be not hindered." (I Peter 3:7) Those who are the most successful with finances are those who have learned the principle of being "heirs together" with decisions in life; sons should be trained in this important concept.

Daughters need vocational training, too. But instead of a career, she needs to be building over the years those needed skills for homemaking and for being a support and encouragement to her husband and children, skills that would not only help her to be able to guide the house, but that would also be a support to her future husband's Christian service. Such skills would include: baking, sewing, gardening, typing, communication skills like writing, home decorating and orderliness, caring for children, etc. Of course, learning to be a cheerful and "joyful mother of children" (Psalm 113:9) is first encountered through being a cheerful daughter and sister in her own home before marriage. Being occupied in her father's house under his supervision and authority, and seeing this as a training ground for her future home, is important for daughters.

A daughter doesn't just learn the quality of being a chaste keeper at home in a few weeks after her marriage day; she is learning this year after year in her own home before marriage. Having a father who "safely trusts in her" will certainly, in many regards, lead to having a husband who safely trusts her and will "praise her," too. (Prov. 31) Remember, one of the best ways to prepare our sons and daughters for marriage is by simply exemplifying to them in our own marriage Godly, Biblical qualities. As we learn Biblical qualities in our marriage, our children and young people will be learning them too.

The Actual Courtship Period

Some may wonder just how long a Courtship Period should last, and this depends on several factors. However, it should be pointed out that the Courtship period is not the time when parents on either side or the young people involved try to work through doubts or try to feel right about the relationship.

Most, if not all, of these fears, feelings and concerns should be worked through and reasonably laid to rest well before the actual courting period begins, although there may always be some minor concerns from all parties involved.

The Courtship Period primarily begins a spiritual bonding period between the couple and the parents on both sides with the couple. It may also be a preparation period vocationally for the young man, and other practical considerations and arrangements may need to be made during this time which could vary the length of the Courtship Period somewhat. There may not be a specific date or time when the courtship officially begins, but once this courtship has been approved and begins, there are a number of experiences to be included in this period of spiritual bonding.

> *The Courtship Period begins a spiritual bonding period between the couple and also the parents on both sides with the couple.*

Dorcas had many heart to heart conversations with her new future mother-in-law; in fact, there were several times when Ben and Dorcas and Mother and I sat down together and talked about things that involve marriage, family life, and parent/in-law relationships. These were very rich and blessed times together. Ben visited his future in-laws for a weekend one time when Dorcas was away, and they had a special time of getting closer (though we had been together as families many times prior to this). During Andy & Betsy's courtship, Andy & Betsy, Betsy's parents, and Marge & I had some family talks and prayer together. The Courtship Period should involve a sufficient number of these times to help parents come to feel comfortable and adjusted to the new situation and the changes this will bring.

Sometimes parents feel very good about a relationship but may have certain fears. For example, the maid's parents may feel very good about a young man but may wonder or need reassurance on how he will provide for his new bride, or at least how he has made plans or is making plans for this. There may be times when a father-in-law assists his future son-in-law in this area. For example, Moses and Jacob worked for their father-in-law for a period of time. Parents of the son may wonder if their future daughter-in-law can guide the home in some regards and if she seems to want to adapt herself to their son's ways. Sometimes the Courtship Period may involve helping young men and ladies work on these and other marriage-related practical areas.

Ben and Dorcas's courtship was only about four months in length, although we had been growing close and familiar with each other's families for about a year before this, and both sides were reasonably comfortable with the character we had seen in each other. Ben was fairly well-prepared vocationally, having his own business and some savings; and similarly Dorcas was prepared with homemaking skills and disciplines. About 4 months of time was involved from the beginning of Ben & Dorcas's courtship & engagement until they were married. With Andy & Betsy, their courtship lasted about 6 months and their engagement lasted another 6 months, for about a total courtship period of a little less than 1 year. Due to the age and maturity of both couples, it didn't seem like a lengthy courtship would be that necessary for them. However, it seems that with some younger couples who have the approval and blessing of authorities, there may need to be a longer Courtship Period involved during which time both the young man and lady would be preparing themselves vocationally and practically for marriage. I am assuming that their spiritual life is in good order, but there may be some needs there, too, like working on marriage-related passages of Scripture such as Eph. 5 and I Peter 3.

During lengthy Courtship Periods (longer than 1 year), there is some concern with the development of youthful passion temptations, particularly if the couple is together frequently, like once or twice a week or more. This is something to be considered. Parents may need to help steer their young people from situations that could invite temptations. Parents on both sides, along with the couple, need to be involved together in deciding how long the Courtship Period should last, and they should help their young people feel a peace about the length of this period. If the marriage is hastily arranged, they could face post-marriage temptations and fears, thinking that they jumped into the situation and should have waited longer.

On the other hand, too lengthy of a Courtship Period may present premarital temptations and doubts, so good communication and an agreement between parents, future in-laws, and the couple should be made in this decision regarding the length of the Courtship Period.

During the Courtship Period, the young couple should begin the important process of becoming one in spirit and heart about life, learning the early steps in becoming "heirs together of the grace of life." (I Peter 3:7) This is an excellent time for the two to learn how to open up their hearts to one another. This openness is vital to a good marriage and is best learned before other things start getting involved. Writing to each other is helpful in beginning this oneness process, but some

> *During the Courtship Period, the young couple should begin the important process of becoming one in spirit and heart about life.*

people are not as skilled in expressing their feelings as well as others in writing. When two families live far apart and are unable to fellowship together on a regular basis, some parents allow letter writing between young people as a Pre-Courtship way of evaluating others. In some circumstances, this may be acceptable, but both young people, here again, should be of sufficient age and maturity before this should begin. The young people should also have parental approval for this, and the letters should be read by both sets of parents before they are sent and when received. The frequency of such writing may need to also be limited somewhat (for example, allowing once-a-month writing or something similar).

If parents are not familiar with the character of the young man involved, it may be best for the young man to first write his future prospective father-in-law or perhaps brothers of the maid rather than the daughter. This should take place until the father is assured of the young man's character. The maid might want to write her future prospective mother-in-law or perhaps the young man's sisters also. Letter writing in the Pre-Courtship Period can lead to emotional involvement and a dating spirit and should be approached cautiously and wisely.

Phone conversations in the Courtship Period are good to build unity and to open up hearts if you can afford it. But as things progress in the Courtship Period and seem to be going well, the couple may need some times together somewhat alone to get acquainted. In addition to our family times together, Ben & Dorcas needed some of these special times together, with just the two of them. They took walks together around our property on Sunday afternoons and shared some times of sitting together alone on the front porch. Andy & Betsy had similar daytime activities they did together.

With Dorcas's family living in Pennsylvania, we would occasionally visit back and forth on weekends; after their courtship began, Dorcas visited our home for several days without her family. Sometimes parents may worry or be cautioned not to allow their young people into any situations where they are alone together. Of course, discernment needs to be used, and if parents have extreme fear regarding this, then the young people probably shouldn't be alone together much; but the basis of that fear may also bring into question the Christian moral integrity of the young people. With Betsy's family living across the country from ours, frequent visits were impractical, so we kept up communication via phone calls, letters, and faxes. Betsy's family flew to Vermont for a visit about 3 months after Andy & Betsy's courtship began, and Andy flew out several times to spend a long weekend with Betsy's family. After 6 months, our 2 families met together in Colorado, and it was during this week long camping trip together as families that Andy & Betsy were engaged.

Chaperoning should be a part of courtship and is another aspect that sets courtship above dating; it will help to minimize the possibility of youthful temptations. Everyone has the potential of being tempted, and we should wisely "make no provision for the flesh to fulfill the lusts thereof." Much of the temptation in this area in the past has happened to those who have a dating mentality where the couple is simply enjoying the companionship and passions of being with another young person without being serious about marriage; many times such a young couple falls into fleshly temptations. But when a young person has the goal of glorifying the Lord with his (or her) own life and with his (or her) future marriage, and has the inner controls that are a part of a good conscience, and when a young person has been raised with a spirit and heart that honors purity and holiness in himself (or herself) and others, then this young person already has inner integrity that will caution him (or her) not to enter into situations that may invite temptation. Furthermore, when a young person has a love for the Word of God and the moral absolutes contained therein, he (or she) will be able to wisely avoid situations that may create youthful passions; he (or she) will "flee youthful lusts". This young person has internally set boundaries - boundaries that are set by conscience, the Holy Spirit, the Word of God, and a desire to love and please God. This young person can be trusted, and the very fact that he (or she) is "going through courtship" enables him (or her) to realize that the Lord has certain blessings for him (or her) that will come only on that future marriage day.

There are many today who do not understand the power of such inner controls because their passions and desires have continually only been restrained by external rules and regulations. External restraints (laws and rules) will not transform the heart nor will they create purity within; in fact, the Scriptures teach that such laws will create all manner of "evil desire (concupiscence)" in the heart. (See Romans 7.) There are also many today who mean well and self-righteously pride themselves in saying such things as, "Our couples have never even touched hands until their marriage day." Often those who glory in a few externals have extreme violations in others ways and have hearts that struggle with lust.

Naomi didn't fear sending Ruth to Boaz' threshing floor; Ruth was to wash and anoint herself and then lay herself down at Boaz' feet during the night. This seemed rather curious morally no matter how one tries to look at the customs of the day. Boaz, himself, said, "Let it not be known that a woman came into the threshing floor." It could have obviously been misconstrued by others. But Naomi was very familiar with both her daughter-in-law's integrity and Boaz' moral integrity; they were Godly, self-controlled, Christian people, and Naomi knew this. Many legalistic Christians today would be the first ones to accuse Ruth and Boaz for some impropriety. Externally set courtship conduct rules can invite self-righteous pride and often manifests itself in a judgmental spirit towards those who have good moral integrity, though externally they do not meet all the prescribed outward requirements. If you are overly worried about your young person's moral life, the time to start working on this is long before courtship; and if he (or she) has some struggles in this area, greater restriction will need to be given to their courtship times together.

We personally do not feel it is good for a young couple to go off together in the evening; this kind of night life can invite temptations. Large groups of teens going off together on different outings or even for ministry purposes could also fall into this category. Participating together as families has a "built-in" chaperoning advantage.

In the very early stages of the courtship period, the young couple should be able to sit together on the porch, or perhaps take a walk to get the mail together, or some other similar daytime errand. As the courtship progresses and there seem to be general good feelings and confidence in the developing relationship, some other opportunities for the young couple to get better acquainted alone may be advisable. Of course, as previously stated, the amount of freedom given here depends on the trustworthiness we have, and this trustworthiness is dependent on the moral integrity of the young people as well as their ages.

We've recently observed two Christian couples in their mid to late twenties who are going through courtship; and it seemed more appropriate for them to have greater amounts of time alone, due to their age and Christian maturity. But both of these couples were sincere, dedicated Christians who knew the foolishness in dabbling in passions, and they could be trusted. However, for a younger couple perhaps in their late teens or early twenties, it would be more advisable and prudent to set limitations on the length and frequency of such times alone.

As the courtship moves into the later months or perhaps into the early days of the engagement period, greater freedom for the couple to be alone can usually be allowed without concern. For example, Ben took Dorcas to the optician and to look for some new glasses frames, and they also had other times of going shopping together during the day. It seems that daytime activities together are far more proper than evening ones, but if either parent on either side of the courtship arrangement has some fears, cautions, or concerns about some of the young couple's activities together, then these warning signals should be promptly heeded. Parents best know the weaknesses of their own children, and God will prompt parents with His Spirit when concerns in the area of youthful temptations are potentially present.

As the engagement period is approached, or when the actual marriage date is set, times together alone will help to build a spirit of oneness and heart to heart communication that is so important to the foundation of a good marriage. Good communication between parents and future in-laws and the couple themselves should all be a part in establishing some guidelines for chaperoning the courtship period of the young couple involved so that everyone feels comfortable about what is proper and God-honoring.

Moral Excellence

While on this subject of moral purity and excellence, how is this best achieved in youth? Will making commitments to moral purity, trying to avoid thinking about boys and girls, etc., or avoiding eye contact with others lead to moral purity? While these things do reflect somewhat of a desire for righteousness on the part of a person for purity, promising or vowing or being determined to make one's self pure becomes largely dependent on our human efforts to achieve it. Sometimes in following human efforts, we succeed in looking right but fail to be truly inwardly transformed in heart or thought life. I would suggest seeking grace for purity within. Grace is God's power to transform lives, and it will bring about a lasting transformation of motives in time.

In a similar manner, avoiding eye contact is an important aspect to showing discretion in actions and conduct, but a girl can be very proper with her eyes and yet be very improper in her independent, free, friendly lifestyle; and the same is true with boys. The "strange woman" in Proverbs was first of all "out and about"; and then next she caught the young man with her eyes. Many are trying to be determined to be pure in thought, but they live in such a world-conformed manner that it becomes very difficult to avoid tempting thoughts and actions. We cannot expect to create inner purity by determinations and commitment to it, and then continually be exposing ourselves to a tempting lifestyle. Paul taught the strengthening values in "making no provision for the flesh to fulfill the lusts thereof." Jesus taught this concept also. He said, "There is nothing from without a man, that entering into him can defile him, but the things which come out of him, those are they that defile the man." "For out of the heart proceed evil thoughts, etc....These are the things which defile a man." (Matt 15:11-20 and Mark 7:14-23)

> *If we can diligently "keep" our children's hearts pure through the teen period, they will not yield or be defiled by evil when they are older.*

If we can diligently "keep" our children's hearts pure through the teen period, they will not yield or be defiled by evil when they are older. The greatest way to strengthen a young man or lady morally is by simple separation and purity in the child-rearing period of their life. Keep them innocent throughout their entire youth. We would suggest avoiding regular teen associations or fellowships; these involvements will soon captivate your young person's thought life. Avoid reading materials, videos, TV and radio programs, and preaching that is constantly addressing the moral sins of this world or where boy/girl talk is frequently the topic. Fellowship with those of pure motives and speech, with those who have proper children, and if you can't find any, stand alone and don't compromise. In the right timing, God will bring you in contact with another Godly family.

Purify your home (you may want to pray about moving out to the country), read only Godly wholesome literature, spend your time in God's Word, take care of the "sheep" and garden, enjoy your family using Biblical child discipline methods, avoid a lot of youth attractions and entertainments, and your young person will reach the age of 18 to 20 with a pure heart, pure motives, contentment, moral integrity and an understanding of what is proper, not only with their eyes but, above all, with their conduct.

What about encouraging your son or daughter to vow or promise in some way that they will not think about boys or girls until they have parental approval? Is this a good idea? I would avoid doing this. Making such promises actually will strengthen the potential for lust and stimulate thoughts in the very area you're trying to avoid. Such promises are like setting a law upon ourselves, and "the law made no man perfect." (Heb. 7:19) Paul said the law will actually create all manner of evil desire in the heart. These promises and vows will tend to do this in a young person's heart. Rather I would follow the above plan of avoiding wrong exposure and developing a routine of evaluating life and others together with your young person. They will respect you and want to stay under your counsel and authority, and they will one day meet their life partner free of a past of lust and longings.

The Engagement or Betrothal Period

After a period of courtship and growing in unity and after seeking our counsel, Ben thought it would be best if he once again asked Dorcas's Father about actually marrying Dorcas. He gave Ben his approval and blessing and, then, Ben offered his formal proposal to Dorcas. Andy approached Betsy's parents in the same way and also received their blessing.

Following this actual proposal, Ben & Dorcas as well as Andy & Betsy were free to publicly announce their engagement and future marriage. In a sense, they were "spiritually married" at this point and began finalizing plans for their future. They then began working together with parents on both sides to arrive at a marriage date that was comfortable and agreeable with all. The date was not set too far in the future to upset the momentum of their plans, and neither was it made too hastily so that there was a wrong sense of anxiousness in it. We did notice that as the actual marriage dates began to arrive, the adversary began to try to throw doubts and fears

> *Whenever God is doing a work, we can expect the adversary to come along with fiery darts and temptations.*

into the situation. Whenever God is doing a work, we can expect the adversary to come along with fiery darts and temptations; you can expect to experience some of this. This Engagement or Betrothal Period was a final bonding time, and much depth of oneness in spirit came about during this period in their lives.

Concluding Thoughts

Finally, in evaluating a potential marriage partner for your son or daughter, do not become overly critical. We homeschooling parents, in general, tend to be ultra discerning and analytical in life; we've had to be this way to protect our children. There will always be little "concerns" that we may have about the character of others; however, by being overly critical, these concerns can often get exaggerated. Bear in mind that some of the changes that take place in a young person's life happen after the marriage. If all the character had to be there prior to marriage, there would be little need for those many sections of Scripture dealing with marriage. Husbands wouldn't need to "wash with the Word" through a "loving and giving spirit," and wives wouldn't need to "win" their saved husbands to the Word through a "meek and quiet" reverent spirit. We have learned that it is very important to consider character, but we have also seen that some of the "concerns" that Dorcas's parents had and some of the "concerns" that we had and some of the "concerns" that Ben and Dorcas had about each other have been inconsequential. They have actually gone the opposite way of our "concerns" after they were married. Marriage will always be the union of two, imperfect human beings to some degree in this life; do not allow the tempter to use normal imperfections to cause you to fear if, in general, you feel pretty good about the developing relationship.

In conclusion, let us remember as the Proverbs say that there are four things that are too wonderful for man, too deep and unfathomable for him to comprehend. One of these is "the way of a man with a maid". (See Prov. 30:18 & 19.) We can involve proper authority structure in arranging a courtship and marriage, and we should. We can evaluate character and commitment and other details in the young person's life, and we should. But let us remember that God has made them "one" in the beginning. God is very much involved in bringing about this union; let us watch for His miraculous working.

Abraham sent his servant to a place where he could find a wife for Isaac who would be of suitable character and commitment. (See Genesis 24.) When Abraham's servant went to the well in Haran, he wanted to see God work a miracle so that he would know that he, in his own strength, hadn't worked things out. Abraham's servant began to pray, "O Lord God of my master Abraham, I pray thee, send me good speed this day, and shew kindness unto my master, Abraham. Behold, I stand here by the well of water; and the daughters of the men of the city come out to draw water: And let it come to pass, that the damsel to whom I shall say, Let down thy pitcher, I pray thee, that I may drink; and she shall say, Drink, and I will give thy camels drink also: let the same be she that thou hast appointed for thy servant Isaac...And it came to pass, before he had done speaking, that, behold, Rebekah came out..." The Scriptures then tell us that Abraham's servant ran to meet her and said, "Let me, I pray thee, drink a little water of thy pitcher...And when she had done giving him drink, she said, I will draw water for thy camels also..."

This was the first miracle involved, the exact answer to his prayers; but one miracle was not enough for this wise servant to be convinced that this, indeed, was the right woman. He then asked an important question to the maid - "Whose daughter art thou? Tell me..." She could very likely have been one of the daughters of the idolatrous men of the regions, and an idolater herself; and, of course, this would have never done for Abraham and Isaac. Her reply was that she was Bethuel's daughter, Milcah's and Nahor's granddaughter. This was the second great miracle; but, here again, this was not enough for this wise servant, for he knew that such miracles had to be validated by the approval of the authorities involved.

Abraham's servant soon proceeded to Rebekah's home where, before eating, he clearly explained the purpose of his coming. He described the miracles at the well, and then inquired of Rebekah's brother Laban and her father Bethuel their feelings about the situation, to which they replied: "The thing proceedeth from the Lord: we cannot speak unto thee bad or good. Behold, Rebekah is before thee, take her and go, and let her be thy master's son's wife, as the Lord hath spoken..." It took two miracles and the approval of authority (which is a miracle in itself) to verify the Lord's leading in this matter. However, it is interesting to note that when there was a debate as to when they should leave (which suggested some doubt arising in the situation), they also inquired of the maid whether she was willing to go. They consulted her feelings over the matter saying, "Wilt thou go with this man? And she said, I will go."

> *Young people must give full consideration to the authorities on both sides ... being sure their parents feel "right" about the relationship.*

Ben & Dorcas kept saying they were going to have to write a book about all the little miracles involved in their lives coming together, but they also had sought approval from their authorities and were of mature, marriageable age. When I told Ben I was going to share this about the miracles, he suggested this caution: "Dad, be sure to tell them not to work up miracles." This is true; young people must give full consideration to the authorities on both sides of a budding relationship, being sure their parents feel "right" about the relationship. Parental approval is somewhat of a miracle in itself and is a major part of the process. Andy & Betsy have testified that they would not be married today if they had not obeyed the counsel of their parents.

Parents need to honestly and wisely sense when it is time for their young person to start considering courtship and when they are truly mature enough for marriage. I have noticed with both of our sons that Marge & I began to feel it was "time" for them to marry just a few months before they began their courtships (both were around the age of 23). Somehow God places this feeling in parents' hearts. We have noticed that many parents start worrying and working at this long before they should, particularly with their first child to marry. When your young person is reasonably prepared in character, commitment, maturity and vocation for marriage, God will bring along a mate who will also be reasonably prepared. God works this way, and when it is all over, you will wonder why you were so concerned about everything.

> *Parents need to honestly and wisely sense when it is time for their young person to start considering courtship and when they are truly mature enough for marriage.*

One final blessing which is a result of courtship is that it will lead to continued close family relationships. It will be only natural for young people who have been close to their parents during their childhood years and the process of courtship to want to continue drawing from parental experience, insight and counsel. It is true that the newlyweds will need to "leave and cleave" (see Ephesians 5:31) and begin formulating to some extent their own unique outlook and approach to life. But when there are wise, God-honoring parents and marriages on both sides from which to draw, your newly married children will learn many marriage skills from you on how to "live joyfully with the wife of their youth all the days of their lives." (Ecclesiastes 9:9) You will be blessed to see your children's children, and this will bring you much joy and satisfaction.

Andy & Betsy's Story

by Andy Barth

God is so good! How we praise Him for all He has done in bringing our two lives together. Ephesians 3:20 has been very meaningful to us from the very beginning of our courtship and even now that we are married: "Now unto Him that is able to do exceeding abundantly above all that we ask or think, according to the power that worketh in us, unto Him be glory."

Our courtship was a blessed experience, and we thank the Lord for how He led our parents and us in this important area of our lives of finding a life partner. We saw God's marvelous working in every detail to bring us together, even though our two families were not close at all geographically - the Barths in Vermont and the Bradricks in Washington state.

Home schooling played a very important role in preparing us for our lives together. We are so grateful that our parents were willing to give their time and energy to train us at home. As a boy, I was able to apprentice under my father in his dental lab, which he had at home. By the time I was 20, I had started my own lab, which I am now operating out of our own home. For this we are grateful. Betsy, the second oldest of nine children, had been taught and had cultivated all the necessary skills of organizing, serving, and caring for a home and family for many years. She now enjoys using those skills in our home. We are thankful that our parents' training in Godly character qualities, such as responsibility, submission, love, and giving ourselves for others, prepared us to fulfill our roles as husband and wife. Of course, being brought up to love and serve the Lord was the best preparation of all. It is a joy to have loving parents who led us to salvation in Jesus Christ.

As Betsy & I were growing older, of course, we each began to wonder, "How am I ever going to meet another Godly young person to marry?" By God's grace, we were able to wait on Him and honor our parents' authority in this area. We were both in our early 20's when our courtship began. After a wonderful courtship and beginning a blessed marriage, we see that God had "someone" perfectly made for each of us. We didn't just happen to finally meet another Godly young person, but God had made, prepared, and kept each of us for the other. He was able to bring us together in His perfect timing as we waited on Him and allowed Him to work through the authority of our parents.

So how did we meet? Both of our families have home schooled for many years and have ministered to other home school families. Our families met at a home school convention in May of 1994 and were blessed to be able to spend an evening together over a meal and a time of sharing and singing. We were surprised to see how God had led us in such similar paths. At that time I hadn't "noticed" Betsy, but the Bradricks were a wonderful big family. Several months later the Lord impressed upon my parents' hearts that perhaps Betsy was the "one" for me. After praying some time about this possibility, they sought my thoughts and heart about it. Over the years the Lord had been teaching me the importance of honoring my parents' counsel, and I was very open to see how God was working through them.

My father then called Betsy's father and asked him what he would think about a relationship developing between the two of us. Mr. Bradrick was a bit surprised, but said that they would pray about it. A number of weeks passed, and after much prayer and a few phone conversations between fathers, parents on both sides began to feel that perhaps this was of the Lord. Through a number of visits between families early in 1995, Betsy's parents had the opportunity to better evaluate me, and, of course, I thought the world of Betsy! When Betsy's parents were completely at peace with this being possibly God's will for their daughter, they spoke with her to see if the Lord might also confirm this in her heart. And He did.

We were both overwhelmed by how God had done exceeding abundantly beyond all we ever thought possible Our parents encouraged us to begin communication, which, for the most part, was writing since we were not together a lot. We soon discovered that both families had fax machines, and by the time of our wedding, we had filled a notebook. We did have many precious opportunities to be together - walking through a park: driving by the lake to see the sunset; doing family projects together; or just sitting, talking, praying, and singing together. It was good to be under authority during our entire courtship and to be able to seek our parents' counsel in all the decisions we made. After several months I asked Mr. Bradrick how they would feel about us becoming engaged. We felt that a good time would be in June as our families met in Colorado for a convention and a week of camping. It was so peaceful knowing that we had our parents' full blessing when I asked Betsy an important question and she said, "Yes."

Later in August after consulting with our parents and families, we decided upon a wedding in late December. There was much to do as I had the privilege of building a house and as Betsy and her family were busy with wedding preparations. We had a simple wedding in Betsy's home with our families sharing and our fathers performing the ceremony. It was a blessing to enjoy each other and all the Lord had done for us rather than giving much attention to details and traditions. We are so happy to have no regrets about our entire courtship & wedding. It was all wonderful. "He hath made everything beautiful in His time." (Eccl. 3:11)

Our encouragement to young people is, first, if you are waiting for a life partner, don't be discouraged by always wondering how or when you will get married. Pour yourself into joyfully serving the Lord in your own home with your parents and family, and wait on God's timing. That will bring you the greatest joy. This is preparation for marriage and for life.

Second, but most important, place yourself totally under your parents' authority. Tell them that you are wanting God to work through them to help you to discern God's best for your life. If Betsy & I hadn't honored our parents, we wouldn't be married today.

Finally, whether you are waiting for a life partner or are in a courtship now, see your courtship and future marriage as very important. Place it in the high and holy position that it is, and seek to please God in all you do; He will bless you.

God has blessed us with a home on some acreage near my family here in a lovely farming valley in Vermont, and we are now enjoying our lives together. Betsy shared a verse with me at the very beginning of our courtship that is one of our favorites. "Except the Lord build the house, they labor in vain that build it." (Psalm 127:1) Truly it is the Lord who has built our relationship, and we know that He is the One who will build our home.

We say with the Psalmist, "Yea, I have a goodly heritage" (Psalm 16:6b), and we look forward, if God so blesses, to teaching and training our little ones someday just as we were taught. We will need God's grace and help each step of the way, but we know that He who has begun a good work in us, will, by His great love and mercy, be faithful to complete it. Praise Him!

Andy & Betsy
December 30, 1995

Andy & Betsy
March 1996

Ben & Dorcas
November 14, 1992

Ben & Dorcas & Peter & Annette
December 1995

Other Writings From Parable Publishing House Which Compliment This Book On Courtship:

Becoming Heirs Together of the Grace of Life
by Jeff & Marge Barth

This 167 page book has in-depth discussions of marital roles which will lead to a most rewarding & fulfilling lifetime of marriage. Many have ordered this book to present as a marriage gift. $6.00

Child Training & the Home School
by Jeff & Marge Barth

True character which will lead to the Godly home & marriage is built through the process of child training. This 164 page book encompasses concepts in proper authority arrangements, methods of child discipline, and Godly social development which are foundational to purity & holiness. $6.00

Indepth Articles by the Barths:

"Key to an Orderly Home" - $1.00
"The Spirit of Modesty" - $1.00
"Preventing & Turning Rebellion in Youth" - $2.00
"Training Children to Honor Parents" - $2.00
"Work Ethics, Apprenticeship, & Home Occupations" - $2.00

Please include $2.00 S&H on above orders.
To order the above items, and for a list of other family materials available, please write to:

Parable Publishing House
RD 2, Box 2002
Middlebury, Vermont 05753